# WHISPERS OF FREEDOM

## ESCAPING THE ORDINARY AND DISCOVERING LIFE'S SECRETS BEYOND THE ECHOES

MOHITH KUMAR ABAKA

# Contents


*Preface* v

*Acknowledgements* vii

  1. The Why 1

  2. A Journey Through Time And Art 3

  3. Where The Rainforest Comes Alive 14

  4. Seaside Encounters And Culinary Delights 22

  5. Where Culture Meets The Coast 30

  6. Waterside Awakening 41

  7. Journeys Beyond, Conversations Within 49

  8. Cafe Chronicles: Conversations Beyond Midnight 55

  9. Homeward Trails 59

Echoes of the Journey 65

# Preface

Have you ever had that itch for an adventure, that craving for the unknown? Well, I've had it for as long as I can remember.

Going on a long solo trip on a bike had been a dream of mine for ages. I've always had a deep love for travel like it's in my blood. To bring it to life, I did all the usual research – mapped out the places to visit, sought advice on where to rest my head, and about all the exciting things I might find.

Although at first, the plan was to go with friends in a small group on bikes. I asked around and planned it out, but it never seemed to work out. Every time, something would come up, and the group plans would fall through. It felt like Destiny was trying to tell me something. Maybe, just maybe, this trip was meant to be a solo adventure.

So, I decided to go solo. I got all my stuff together, and it wasn't my first time (I'd done a few short solo trips before, mostly using public transport). This time, though, I'd be on a motorcycle, so I needed some extra gear like basic tools and a first-aid kit.

In the days before I left, I had this weird mix of feelings. It was kind of like the nerves you get before a big interview or doing something huge. I guess it's because I'd been thinking about this day for so long.

This book is about that journey. It's about the thrill of hitting the open road, feeling the wind on your face, and not knowing what's around the next bend (no matter what you plan, destiny always has something for you in place and that is the most beautiful thing about solo travel). I hope you'll come along with me on this adventure, and maybe, it'll inspire you to embark on your own.

# Acknowledgements

You know, I was the kind of guy who used to dream big while doing science homework (why should math have all the fun? xD). It was a pretty ordinary existence until I decided, "Why not make life a little extra-ordinary?" So here's to adding a pinch of spice to the regular masala! As I embark on this journey through the pages of this book, there are many hearts to whom I owe gratitude and appreciation.

Amma, Nanna and Thammudu [cc: Mom, Dad, and Brother]

First up, my amazing parents - thanks for not panicking (too much) when I declared I was going on this trip. Your unwavering support, love, and guidance have been the compass that directed my dreams. Your unshakable belief in me is like Ross's obsession with dinosaurs; I can't see it, but I know it's a part of who I am, quietly supporting my dreams. And a big shout-out to my younger brother for adding his own touch of joy and curiosity to our family.

Destiny and Nature: The Dynamic Duo

Thank you both for all life's twists and turns, the moments of serendipity, and the beauty of the natural world that shaped my journey in countless ways. You are like the best-worst improv team I've ever met. Keep it up; you make life interesting.

Friends

To my dearest friends, and my partners in mischief, you've shared in the dreams and doubts that led me to this book. Remember when you thought I was kidding about writing a book? Well, the joke's on you. Thanks for all the laughs and disbelief; it was my secret motivation. Jokes apart... there is nothing much to say about you now; I'll move on.

Everyone I've met in life

To everyone I crossed paths with, thank you for being a part of my story. You've left a piece in my heart (and sometimes, my sanity). Thanks for connecting with me, for better or worse. It's like we have a cosmic silver string that keeps us tangled in the messiness of life.

The trip friends

I am thankful to everyone, but special thanks to Adithya, Anushka, Emima, Kanchi, Raji, Sri Ram, and Tharun, for making this trip extra special.

You... Yes, You!

It is to you, dear reader, that I owe the most profound debt of gratitude. You hold this book in your hands (or e-book on your mobile, tab, or laptop xD), and by doing so, you hold a piece of my heart and soul. You grant life to these words and bring meaning to my experiences. Thank you for sharing your journey with me and allowing my story to become a part of your own.

In a world that constantly evolves, I've learned that the mysteries of nature are a powerful force. It has taught me that patience, resilience, and a belief in the unseen can conjure magic from the seemingly ordinary. And if, by some twist of fate, your wishes weren't granted, it's only because destiny has something even greater in store.

I was going to wrap this up with all those fancy words like "deepest gratitude" and "heartfelt appreciation." But, you know what? I thought this suits us better:

With a wink, a grin, and endless thanks,
Mohith Kumar

# CHAPTER ONE

# The Why

Why do I choose solo travel? It's a question I've been asked countless times. "Why Solo? Are you sure?" "Won't it be boring?" "Isn't it dangerous?" "Don't you feel lonely?" "Isn't it costly?" These are just a few of the many doubts people often express when they hear about my solo travel plans.

But let me tell you, solo travel is far from boring. It's a unique opportunity to enjoy your own company and reflect on some of the most important decisions of your life. It's a chance to embrace what I call "self-time" in a world that's often consumed by routine (wake at your mobile-eat-work-eat-work-look at your mobile-sleep-wakeup again).

Solo travel provides a distinct opportunity to connect with the world in a way that is profoundly different from your daily life, and this holds true regardless of your choice of lodging, whether it be hostels, homestays, or luxury resorts. It gives you a fresh perspective and a renewed appreciation for the people and places around you (which most people forget or ignore these days).

Now, let's talk budget. Traveling isn't just for the wealthy. In fact, it's amazing how far you can go with very little money. You can choose from three budget plans: low, mid-range, and high. Each budget opens up a different world of possibilities and experiences, and the same destination can feel entirely different across various budget levels.

The lowest budget: I remember the time we approached truck drivers, seeking a lift on the highways to reach our destination. We even offered to work as volunteers in exchange for a meal and a place to sleep in a few places. This way, we had the chance to meet fellow backpackers, sharing a day with the most minimal budget possible.

Mid-range: For most travelers, this budget is the sweet spot. You stay in hostels, cozy homestays, or comfortable hotels and explore the area in either a rented or personal vehicle. It's the perfect balance, allowing you to make new friends on the road, including those traveling on a tighter budget.

Luxury travel: Some seek the pinnacle of extravagance, choosing to stay in lavish resorts where every detail is designed for comfort. This is by no means a wrong choice; if it makes you feel rejuvenated, allows for introspection, and keeps you balanced, then go for it.

Lastly, safety is of utmost importance for solo travelers. It's not a one-size-fits-all topic; it depends on where you go and how you get there. Here are a few tips of many, for safe solo travel:

1. Use public transport when possible; it's not only economical but also safer.

2. Carry basic repair gear and a first aid kit, and do your research on the destination's suitability for solo travel before reaching there.

3. Keep your family and/or friends informed about your next destination and current status.

4. Avoid traveling after 7:00 PM, stay within your immediate surroundings, and, if you get very bored, take a nap. If you decide to go out, keep it within a very minimal distance around the place where you stay.

5. Know about the local customs and traditions, especially with respect to dressing while visiting any religious places.

6. This is something that you might overlook sometimes, but make sure your gadgets are charged and carry a power bank if possible (During one of my trips, around 6:30 PM, I found myself about 80 km away from my destination with no battery power or power bank. Fortunately, luck was on my side as I spotted a car heading to my destination, and I followed it).

These tips are suggestions I've gathered from local travel experiences, as I haven't ventured outside India myself. But hopefully, that journey will start soon. As I look back, I can't help but think about the incredible adventures that await. Why wait? Let's not keep this adventure all to myself; it's too much fun for one person. So, come on, grab your imaginary backpack, pack your sense of humor, and let's embark on this incredible adventure together. I promise it's going to be a wild ride!

# CHAPTER TWO

# A Journey through Time and Art

The morning sun lit up the sky as I revved my trusty motorcycle. I was feeling a mix of excitement and butterflies in my stomach, but first things first, I had to stop at Veena Stores for a delicious breakfast. There, I tried idly and Vada, and let me tell you, the coconut chutney was a delightful surprise. It was a nice change from the usual peanut chutney I'm fond of.

**Breakfast Bliss @Veena's**

With breakfast behind me, I hit the road. The route through Hassan promised a scenic journey. My first destination was Belur, a chapter in my unfolding adventure. Pulling into Belur, I parked my bike by the Chennakesava temple, right next to a charming little shop. I left my shoes outside and stepped into the temple.

The stone paths echoed as I walked to the impressive Chennakesava temple. It had stood for over 900 years, a testament to time's passage. Belur, the first capital of the Hoysala dynasty, had seen history unfold over the centuries. This temple was really something special. It took three generations to complete this beauty. I couldn't help but be amazed by the intricate carvings covering every inch of the structure. What's more, they built this temple without any cement or binder.

Miniature temple-like structures graced the entrance and inside, the air was filled with the scent of incense, and soft chants echoed around me. The main sanctum was filled with beautifully carved pillars and each pillar told its unique story. It was astonishing to see one pillar that served as an index for all the temple's sculptures. This pillar had a carving of all the different sculptures that were carved on the temple.

After some quiet reflection, I left the temple and collected my shoes, giving a small sum at the footwear stand. My journey continued, taking me from Belur to Halebeedu. The weather was ideal, and the natural beauty around me added to the pleasure of the ride. The smooth roads welcomed my bike, and in the distance, I spotted windmills, adding a touch of charm to the landscape.

**Sacred Serenity @Belur**

As I rode through the lush green trees along the road, Halebeedu greeted me with a gentle drizzle. I parked my bike in front of the temple near a playground. It was peak afternoon when I ventured inside. The area had a free stand for footwear, so I left my shoes behind.

As I walked in, I noticed some broken stones that looked like sculptures on my right, while the temple was on my left. I decided to explore the temple first. In the park, there was a large Shivlinga beside the temple. The architecture, personally speaking, was just as breathtaking as Belur's.

The temple's walls were covered in carvings of gods, goddesses, and scenes from everyday life. This temple was larger in scale compared to Belur and took nearly 190 years to complete. Halebeedu served as the capital of the Hoysalas after Belur.

Here, two temples stood side by side: the Hoysaleshwara and Shantaleshwara temples. Two "Nandi" statues and two Shiva temples right next to each other – a sight I had never seen before. The temple is a twin temple dedicated to Hoysaleshwara and Shantaleshwara, embodying masculine and feminine aspects. I entered the temple through Shantaleshwara temple and noticed that the ceiling had "astadikpalakas" intricately carved on it.

I then proceeded to the Hoysaleshwara temple, and its entrance was a work of art in itself. The main linga stood inside. I prayed and came out to admire the beautiful carvings. The level of detail in the architecture was amazing, and it was hard to believe it was done by hand. The temple had carvings of Puranas and Upanishads, and I was told that 17 out of 18 Puranas were depicted on its walls.

Afterward, I got my shoes and visited a display of broken sculptures a bit further away (the one that I saw by my left while entering). Many remnants of the temple were showcased by the archaeological society, reminding me of the city's name – Halebeedu, which means "ruined city." It was said that the temples near Dorasamudra, a prominent water body in the city, were destroyed by human vandalism.

I walked a bit more and came across what appeared to be a temple-like structure in the distance. I approached it feeling like an explorer of ancient ruins. My imagination ran wild as I approached. "Could this be a secret temple guarded by mystical forces?" I wondered. But, as I got closer, I confirmed that it was indeed a temple – the "Hucheswara temple." Unfortunately, it lay in ruins, with only the base remaining, consisting of about 8-9 layers.

Timeless Stone Poetry @Halebeedu Main Temple - 1

Timeless Stone Poetry @Halebeedu Main Temple - 2

**Main Temple entrance and Hucheswara temple ruins**

I took a walk around and could see no one around there. While I was busy admiring the exquisite architecture around me, my rumbling tummy reminded me that I needed something more substantial. I recalled a tip from my colleague to try "Itihakala," a vegetarian restaurant which was a mere 700 meters from the temple.

Amidst the lush fields and rustic charm, Itihakala appeared before me. The aroma of wholesome, home-cooked food filled the air. I decided to dig in and ordered two chapatis, an ample portion of rice, and the pièce de résistance – a piping hot Holige [a traditional sweet] served with a dollop of ghee. I couldn't help but chat with the owner, who was from Mysore – a city that held a special place in my heart, as I'd spent my graduation days there.

With a contented stomach, I continued my journey to Chikmaglur, even though I'd been there several times in the past few months. I decided to use Chikmaglur as a resting point for my next adventure. In the early evening, I arrived in Chikmagalur. The first thing on my mind was coffee. I picked up some coffee packets at Panduranga Coffee Works, which, by the way, is the place for coffee lovers (a must-try place! Estd. in 1938). I couldn't resist trying a local coffee shop, and I took a sip of their brew.

**Unleashing Culinary Canvas @Itihakala and Crafting Coffee Moments @Panduranga Coffee Works**

With the coffee energizing me, I realized that it was time to search for a place to stay for the night. I headed to the Hosteller, hoping to get a room, but they had no vacancies. Just as I was about to leave, the receptionist stopped me and said, "There was a group of six friends who booked the dorm. One of them can't make it. I'll check with them, and if he's a no-show, you can take that bed." I agreed and waited.

During the wait, I took a short stroll around the campus, listening to the charming sounds of woodpeckers. Soon, a guy from the friends group showed up, and I was welcomed to stay. I checked into the dorm, took a quick shower, and noticed another guest working on his laptop on the bed diagonally across from mine. I introduced myself - I'm Mohith, and he said he was Aditya.

Aditya told me he was from Hyderabad (hey! my hometown!), but I was in for a surprise when he confessed he didn't speak Telugu, the native language of Hyderabad; he was actually from Chennai, Tamil Nadu, and was now working in Hyderabad. We began conversing in Tamil (yes! I speak Tamil), a familiar way to connect with friends from Tamil Nadu, and a preference for watching Tamil movies.

With the evening plans set, I set off for Kallathgiri Falls, which I had not visited in my recent trips to Chikmaglur, and to my disappointment, there was less water than expected. In the monsoon, crossing the waterfall to reach the Veerabhadreshwara temple was impossible. Things had changed since my last visit. As I explored, I unexpectedly ran into Aditya at the temple. I wasn't quite sure if it was him from a distance, but his enthusiastic wave confirmed his identity.

**On the way to Hosteller [The right most picture]; Me in akward pro selfie level @hosteller; and two pictures from Kallathgiri Falls**

As we met, he suggested, "Why don't we head to Kemmangundi to catch the sunset?" I thought it sounded like a great idea and off we went to the hilltop. The area has undergone significant development since my last visit. Benches were set up for visitors to relax, and some parts of the hill were now restricted. We watched the sun dip behind the mountains as the clouds grew darker, promising rain. I was amused at the shades of green around me (I am not certain that I will ever witness such vast shades of green again), providing a deep sense of tranquility. I don't remember the last time I felt so at peace. The mountainous surroundings, the trees, the crisp air, and the impending rain created a profound moment.

**Sunset's silent spectacle @Kemmengundi**

Soon, it was dark, and I typically avoid being out too late when I'm not near my place of stay during travel. As a safety precaution, I urged us to leave. Our destination was nearly 70 kilometers away. The challenge was that my bike didn't have fog lights, a situation I meant to fix, but that's another story.

The dark journey began with me following Aditya. The lack of lights was unnerving, and my bike's narrow headlight made it even more challenging. I missed him a couple of times on the road because of the cars in between. However, I was able to catch up with him sooner. After a few minutes, I stopped to answer a call from my mom. It was clear that I wouldn't catch up to Aditya in this darkness, and it wasn't safe to speed through the Ghats. I was not able to see the edges of the road clearly. So, I decided to take it slow.

As I was about 7 kilometers away from the hostel, Aditya called me. "Bro, you just passed me. I've been waiting for you here for dinner." I backtracked and found him. We decided to dine at a local shop and enjoyed 2 dosas each with potato curry and sambar. It was 9:30 when we returned to the hostel. I greeted people sitting around a bonfire and quickly took off to the dorm.

Feeling tired from the day's adventure, I put my phone on charge, took a quick shower, and drifted into a deep sleep. The alarm was set for 4:30 AM; the plan was to head to Charmadi Ghat for a breathtaking sunrise, followed by a stay in Agumbe for the night.

While in Chikmagalur, you can also visit the captivating Baba Budangiri Hills, explore the enchanting Manikyadhara Falls, and discover the rich history and culture at the Coffee Museum. Nature enthusiasts will be thrilled by the serene beauty of Hebbe Falls and the adventurous Kemmangundi-Z Point Trek. Don't forget to experience the diverse wildlife at the Bhadra Wildlife Sanctuary and sunset at Ayyanakere Lake and Hirekolale Lake.

# CHAPTER THREE

# Where the Rainforest Comes Alive

I woke up early, at 4:30 AM, as my alarm began ringing, and I stepped outside, eager to witness the sunrise. The surroundings were cloaked in darkness, so I decided to spend some time in peaceful contemplation. I discovered a serene spot in the woods, enveloped by the melodious sounds of woodpeckers. Sitting there for 45 minutes was soothing and refreshing.

Upon returning to my room, I freshened up and prepared for another day of adventure. I was craving a delicious benne [cc: butter] dosa, but when I arrived at the Town Canteen, it wasn't available. To fully embrace the Agumbe morning, I settled for a Kesari bath and coffee before setting off for my much-anticipated destination, Agumbe.

**bye-bye selfie @Hosteller; Morning view on the street; and @Town Canteen pictures**

Initially, I had planned to take the scenic route via Charmadi Ghat, but friends who had recently been there informed me that there wasn't much water, and also, it would add about 100 kilometers to the journey. So, I chose to skip Charmadi Ghat this time.

The roads were a joy to ride, so enchanting that I didn't feel like rushing. There were moments when I just wanted to park my bike and soak in the beauty, to be still and do nothing. In fact, if given a chance, I might consider staying there forever; it was that captivating. The roads were largely empty during this part of my journey.

During my ride, I met two adorable companions whom I named Dug and Alpha (you'd recognize if you've seen the movie "Up"). They were initially hesitant but quickly became my best friends when I offered them some biscuits.

As I continued, it seemed like the mountains were in a deep slumber, covered with a foggy blanket. Along the way, I even spotted a peacock, but it eluded my camera. Nevertheless, I captured the memory in my heart (well, technically brain).

**Enjoying the nature's tranquil masterpiece in mist on the way to Agumbe**

It was as though I was hypnotized by nature, driving without a care in the world. I reached "Doddamane" in Agumbe, the very house made famous by "Malgudi Days - Swami and his friends." I had cherished this show as a child and used to watch it with my dad on Sundays.

I navigated to the house's location via Google Maps, but upon arrival, all I saw was the house covered by a tent and a small entrance. I hesitated, wondering if I should enter, uncertain of the actual homestay's location. Someone passing by confirmed that I had indeed reached the homestay. I inquired if I could enter, and he explained that the house was now occupied, and visitors could only see the verandah (a roofed, open-air hallway, attached to the outside of a building).

Seeing "Swami's" home brought immense joy. The person who allowed me to observe the house later joined me. We struck up a conversation, and he introduced himself as Ravi Kumar. While talking, we noticed a leech inching toward his leg. Ravi shared that leeches have an enzyme that acts as an anesthetic (I guess he was talking about hyaluronic acid) and that they also have the capacity to sense blood. To demonstrate, he altered the position of his leg, and we watched as the leech changed its direction. It was a fascinating glimpse for me!

**Clicks @Doddamane, Agumbe. Special mention: Mr. Leech in the circle**

Before leaving, Ravi recommended a visit to Kundadri Hills, emphasizing its must-see status. I checked Google and realized I had passed it. With a sense of adventure, I decided to double back and explore.

Google indicated that I had arrived, but the actual location was about two kilometers away. The place felt remote, with few people around. At the entrance, there was only a gatekeeper, who inquired about my home state and any plastic items or alcohol I might be carrying (It's a plastic-free zone, and they discourage drinking). I reached the end of the path, where I found a flight of steps. The view from the top of the hill was simply fantastic. I couldn't resist taking a few pictures. Only one other couple was there, and the crater-like formations on the hill filled with water added to the scenic charm.

A 17th-century Jain temple was also on the hill, and I took a moment to offer my prayers. As I wandered on the hill, I was reminded of a senior from my university, Dr. Ravi, who now worked at MAHE (Manipal Academy of Higher Education and Research). On a whim, I called him and asked if it was possible to visit him that day and stay until the next. He graciously agreed, and it was a spontaneous plan.

**Nature whispering magic @Kundadri Hills**

With Doddamane unavailable for a stay, this turned out to be a better option. I set out on Agumbe Ghats, also known as the "Queen of Ghats." I was spellbound by the beauty of nature. At that moment, all I wished for was rain. Imagining the rain brought immense happiness to my heart. I was captivated by the stunning scenery. If you ever have the opportunity to travel, experiencing Agumbe Ghat during the monsoon is a must.

I made a brief stop at the Agumbe viewpoint to take in the incredible vistas. The last time I felt this connected to nature was during a visit to Kukke, another destination in Karnataka. Agumbe Ghat had me captivated like no other. The drive was so fascinating that I couldn't pull over for photos.

**Clicks @Agumbe View Point**

Finally, I got to Coin Circle where Ravi had asked me to call him from, which I did. Many of my friends and colleagues were from MAHE, so I took a few photos to share with them, letting them know I was close to their campus. Ravi arrived, and we headed to his home, situated in the staff quarters at Manipal.

As I entered the house, the aroma of biryani filled the air. There were two energetic and delightful children at the home. Following lunch, Ravi and I reminisced about our college days and mutual friends. We enjoyed a brief nap, although it felt like an evening in the blink of an eye.

The evening was delightful, and we visited Manipal Park, which was quite extensive. We observed a few people strolling in the park and explored the area. My favorite spot was a place where you could watch the sunset. There were two benches, and the view unfolded in this sequence: first the trees, then the city's buildings, followed by the distant shoreline, and the setting sun. It reminded me of the movie "Up."

**Manipal park road, staff quarters, and a quick selfie**

Just as the rain started to fall, we found shelter beneath a tree. When it turned into a light drizzle, we decided to head back. We returned home, and I had an amazing egg dosa for dinner. I rested on the bed reflecting on the profound beauty of the day, the simplicity of nature, and the incredible experiences I had encountered.

As I went to sleep, I also thought about the changes I had made to my plans. I didn't go to Charmadi Ghat, and I stayed in Agumbe instead. It made me wonder if destiny had a hand in guiding my choices. Maybe certain things are just meant to be, and there's no escaping them. We often believe that we make decisions in the brief moments when choices present themselves, but what if destiny already knows where it wants to take us, and we're simply acting out those moments based on its will?

# CHAPTER FOUR

# Seaside Encounters and Culinary Delights

The next day started with a beautiful morning, and I was up early, excited about the adventures awaiting. After a refreshing bath, I got ready to visit the Udipi Sri Krishna Temple.

Standing in line with fellow devotees, I patiently awaited the temple's opening. The moment was serene, with the temple pond's tranquil beauty captivating my senses. As I stood there, I couldn't help but notice the melodious chants of mantras filling the air, creating a harmonious backdrop to the spiritual anticipation. I learned that, until the "Mahapooja" was performed later in the day, it was customary not to wear a sleeveless vest within the temple complex.

When I entered, I noticed carvings with Sanskrit and Kannada slokas. There were also outdoor idols of gods. Unfortunately, my temple visit felt rushed because I was pushed ahead by the temple staff.

Leaving the temple, I explored smaller shrines around it within a 200-meter radius. It was now around 8:26, and the sun was still sleeping, casting a serene gloom over the day.

**Divine embrace @Udupi**

I went back to the home to collect my luggage. The children had gone to school, and Ravi was getting ready for work. We wanted to share breakfast because we weren't sure when we'd meet again, but Ravi had a class at 9:30. So, I waited in his office and planned the rest of my day. I decided to visit Malpe, Kapu, St. Mary's Island, and head to Murudeshwar at night.

Ravi returned earlier than expected, and we went for breakfast at the Mandvi Emerald complex. After a hearty meal, I set off for Malpe. I could smell the salty sea air from a few kilometers away.

I first visited the harbor, a bustling place filled with fishing boats and the tales of the sea. There was a lively mix of colors and sounds as fishermen went about their work. It felt like I was part of a maritime opera.

Next, I headed to a Malpe beach walk. I sat on a bench and enjoyed the peaceful sound of the waves. There were only a few people around, and the soothing rhythm of the waves had a calming effect on me.

I walked to the end of the walk and stepped onto the rocky outcrop, where I asked a kind couple to take a photo of me. I thanked the friendly stranger for the picture, which turned out great.

**Tales of harbour and rhythmic waves @Malpe**

Then, I went to the beach, but I found out it was closed from June to September due to high tides. I had a chat with a coast guard who told me about the interesting things they find on the shore, like washed-up objects and sadly, occasionally, washed-up dead bodies.

He mentioned a big blue whale skull they had stored nearby. I got excited about seeing it. I thanked him and headed to the place. The place wasn't far, and the journey offered a beautiful view with a bridge in the middle. The river resembled a graceful neck, adorned with trees like lustrous pearls along the shoreline. It was not a typical tourist spot, but there were steps where you could sit and enjoy some quiet time.

I decided it was time to go back to the city for a special lunch at the 'Ajja-Ajji' hotel. I had seen this place in a YouTube video, and it was run by an old couple who cooked and served the food themselves. I also saw a boat-shaped church on the way and made a quick visit.

**Two quick visit clicks**

When I reached the hotel, Ajji welcomed me with a warm smile. She served food to people across the table, showing a passion for what she does. I was keenly looking at her serve food with so much compassion. She advised me not to think too much and just enjoy my meal. She even noticed I hadn't washed my banana leaf and kindly washed it for me, which made me feel like a child in front of a grandma.

She asked me what I wanted to eat, and I chose the traditional South Indian meal. The food included white rice, various curries, fried dishes, sambar, rasam, pickles, curd, buttermilk, and papad. It was a symphony of flavors on a simple banana leaf.

While paying, she asked where I was from, and I told her Hyderabad. She asked if I was a student of Manipal, but I surprised her by saying I was on a solo trip. She wished me well. I could not talk to Ajja more. While leaving, both of them agreed to take a photo with me. You can see in the picture how quickly Ajja turned his attention to someone who asked for more rice.

**No caption needed; the picture is perfect**

With heart and mind both full, I continued to Kapu Beach, where I sat on a bench. There were only a few school students playing nearby. A rope signaled that the beach was off-limits, though the guard was lenient, letting people play near the waves. He told me the rope was for the evening when the tides got higher.

So, my original plan was to hit the beach first and then head to Murudeshwar in the evening. But here's the kicker: the lighthouse on the beach, the one I was so pumped to climb for a killer sunset view, was shut tight. Apparently, it's a night owl and only opens up at 5:30 PM. On top of that, my headache was really starting to crash the party. So, what's a weary traveler to do? I decided to ditch the grand plan, roll with the punches, and stay the night right there. Sometimes, you gotta let go and let the universe surprise you, right?

So there I was on the beach, binging 'F.R.I.E.N.D.S' and realizing the day was slipping away. Suddenly, the thought hit me—I needed a place to crash for the night. Thank the stars for Google! A quick search led me to this homestay called 'Amma Prema,' just a stone's throw away. I decided to give them a call. Mr. Prashanth, the owner, answered and, after a bit of haggling for a sweet deal, bam—my stay for the night was sorted.

**A long-wait afternoon @Kapu Beach**

After completing the paperwork, Mrs. Kasthuri Prashanth offered me a few excellent food recommendations. The homestay featured a lovely backyard with hammocks, swings, and a collection of pets, including dogs, ducks, and cats. Arjun, one of the dogs, was very friendly, so we took a walk together. However, my headache was worsening, prompting me to return to the room where I eventually fell asleep.

I woke up at 6:10 and went back to the lighthouse to enjoy the view, as the evening sky was so beautiful that I couldn't resist it. I went to the rocks where the lighthouse was, and time flew by as I took in the view. I wanted to go up to the lighthouse, but it was already closed. It's only open for 45 minutes, from 5:50 to 6:15.

I went back to my spot on the rocks and took a short nap. When I woke up, the shoreline was beautifully lit. I went to have dinner at a beach shack, where I was the only customer. It felt like having a private beach. After dinner, I went back to my room. While searching for rooms in Murudeshwar, I found 'Trinity Villa Homestay' with good reviews and next to a backwater boating place. I called the owner, Mr. Oliver and we agreed on a fair price. With all my arrangements in place, I settled in for the night.

**Snack time pictures with my friends**

**Wave-made-wow moments + Arjuns love + Yum...slurp!**

A mysterious sound outside my room broke the stillness after a few minutes, resembling someone walking on an iron staircase. Curiously, I glanced at the time; it was almost 11 PM. I hesitated, waiting to see if someone would knock at my door, yet no one did. Gathering my courage, I decided to investigate the source of the sound.

I cautiously creaked open the door, and to my relief, I found Arjun outside. It was raining, and he probably didn't know where to go. We sat for a while, and when the rain turned into a drizzle, I dropped him off at the entrance of the home and went back to sleep.

After a tiring day, I drifted into a deep slumber, comforted by the gentle drizzle and the soothing sound of the waves.

# CHAPTER FIVE

# Where Culture Meets the Coast

The next morning, I had the best start to my day. I woke up to the soothing sound of the waves and the melodious 'suprabhatham' chants from a nearby house around 4:15. I peered out the window, catching a glimpse of the waves crashing, and the gentle drizzle still lingered. In the soft blue morning light, I went out to sit by the shore. The rain intensified, forcing me to return indoors. It was too heavy to continue my journey, so I decided to take a quick nap.

About half an hour later, I woke up, and the rain had eased off. I got ready and left the key in the window as I had promised Prashanth. I then set off towards Marvanthe Beach. The road was a delight, and despite my strong urge to capture pictures, the persistent drizzle and the desire to not miss the sunrise at Marvanthe Beach kept me from doing so.

I made a pit stop at Akshatha near Udupi for breakfast. Even though I'm not a fan of Upma, I was told that their Upma was delicious, and it certainly was. With a content stomach, I continued my journey to Murudeshwar. The route was dotted with picturesque bridges that were impossible to resist. I clicked pictures at three or four different spots, including a fantastic shot of a bird in flight.

Nature exceeded my expectations, and the beauty was beyond what I'd imagined. Usually, things in life aren't as good as we picture them, but with nature, it's often even better. The views were breathtaking. The rain picked up again, and it was everything I'd imagined: a bike ride in the rain amidst lush greenery. I lowered my speed and lifted my helmet visor, enjoying the raindrops on my face.

While on the road, I encountered a sad sight – a dog had been hit and didn't make it. My mood soured; it was the second such incident on this trip, the first being on the way from Agumbe to Manipal. Here, I'd like to share some tips on how to avoid accidents involving dogs while driving on highways:

1. This tip is not only for animal safety but also yours. Always maintain a safe speed so that you have control of the vehicle.

2. Keep an eye on the sides of the road where dogs may be present. Especially in the village/town limits.

3. When you notice the presence of the animals on the road, honk to alert them.

4. If you spot a dog or an animal near the road, slow down and give it space.

Please also refrain from making abrupt lane changes to avoid dogs. These actions could lead to more significant accidents with other vehicles.

The rain intensified, and I had to take a break. I sat beside a small pool of water by the road, on the footpath. A passing truck splashed water on me, which was quite the spectacle, similar to what you might see in some Instagram videos.

When I was about 10 kilometers from Marvanthe, my excitement grew. I was more thrilled about Marvanthe than I had been about Agumbe, although I'm not sure why. Finally, I reached my destination.

I parked my bike and walked over to the rocky shore, where I spent nearly an hour just sitting there, taking in the tranquil surroundings. I took some fantastic photos of the waves crashing against the rocks, even using a timer for some shots. The soothing sound of the waves provided the perfect backdrop for my quiet contemplation.

## Sea breeze whispers @Marvanthe

After my time at Marvanthe Beach, I continued my journey to Murudeshwar. I arrived at the temple, and the view of the Shiva statue was incredible. Half of the statue was visible, with the temple gopuram partially covering the other half. The temple had a powerful spiritual ambiance. I left my bag and sandals and entered for darshan. Unfortunately, I had no small change to leave with them, which meant I couldn't leave my things behind. If you plan to visit, make sure you have some 10 rupee notes with you.

The darshan was quick, taking just about 15 minutes. Around the main temple, there were smaller temples dedicated to Vinayaka, Subramanya, and Parvathi. I visited them before noticing a door on the left that led to the massive Shiva statue, the second largest in India. There was also a cave where they narrated stories from the Shiva Purana, but there was a 50-rupee charge to enter. Additionally, there was a shrine dedicated to Shanishwara. I visited that and started back.

**In awe of Shiva's majestic presence @Murudeshwar**

I had initially planned to go to the top of the temple gopuram for a panoramic view, but the line was quite long, and I was informed that the operators responsible for the lift and ticket issuance would be leaving for lunch shortly. This would entail a three-hour wait, which I couldn't afford. Collecting the small change I needed to retrieve my bag and sandals proved to be a bit of a challenge, as nobody seemed willing to provide it.

Afterward, I went to a near by hotel and requested cash for an amount I intended to send via phone pay. They were kind enough to provide the coins, and I reclaimed my belongings. As I was leaving the restaurant, I remembered to call Oliver and let him know I was on my way. He assured me that lunch would be ready when I arrived.

Upon reaching his place, I found that his home was located right beside the Sharavathi backwaters, offering a picturesque view. It was a warm family home, with the ground floor serving as their residence and the first floor having two homes for rent.

After a refreshing shower and a change of clothes, Oliver had sent me a list of nearby restaurants, recommended one restaurent, and the dishes to try there. The best part was that they would deliver the food to the home. I ordered squid pepper dry and egg fried rice. The food was delivered around 11:30 AM, and I lay down on the bed after eating, eventually drifting off to sleep, still unaware of how exhausted I was.

**Lunch with my favorite guests - calories!**

Welcome to the second half of the day, a time of tides and tranquility. I woke up and headed to Apsarakonda Beach. There was a wedding photoshoot happening on the coast, and I couldn't resist taking a picture of the lovely couple. Cheers to their bright future!

I spent some time on the beach, capturing timer pictures of myself with the photography props scattered along the shore. Then, I started to walk towards Apsarakonda cliff. The terrain was steep and quite perilous. After some effort, I reached the point, and the view was nothing short of amazing.

As I explored further, I noticed some people ascending a set of steps that seemed to lead somewhere interesting. I inquired and learned they were headed to the top of a hill for a better view. I decided to follow the steps, despite the presence of caterpillars, snails, and leeches along the way. The view however, was somewhat obstructed by trees, offering only a limited glimpse of the beach through a couple of gaps. Despite this, the journey through nature was a worthwhile experience.

**@Apsarakonda Beach picture dump; Cheers to the couple (left most picture)**

Next, I made my way to Apsarakonda Falls. These falls were truly spectacular, providing a mesmerizing sight. There was a marked boundary, warning against crossing due to the depth on the other side. However, a wedding photoshoot was taking place in the available space, limiting my movement. This waterfall remains unspoiled by human interference, making it as pristine and magnificent as it can be. Nestled within a small forest, these falls evoke Bali vibes, satisfying the desire for a tropical paradise.

**OOPS!**

I only have the videos of this place and this is the only available picture. This is the result of me trying to exclude the photoshoot and the marked boundary in the picture.

**This place is always better in real than the pictures!**

After enjoying my time there, I proceeded to the Sharavathi Kandla Mangrove Boardwalk. The mangrove forest was a soothing sight. Walking along the beautiful wooden walkway amidst lush green mangrove trees was a wonderful way to connect with nature and find tranquility.

A few information boards were set up to educate visitors about the flora and fauna of the mangrove forests. Crossing the wooden bridge, I found myself surrounded by the backwaters of the Sharavathi River, with scenic water and greenery all around. Moving on, I reached a wooden path that meandered through the mangroves, offering a chance for wonderful photographs. It's important to be cautious about the gaps in the path, especially when walking with children or carrying keys and mobile devices.

Now, let's learn a bit about mangroves: Mangroves are woody plants or plant communities that thrive in the intertidal zones, where land and sea meet, experiencing periodic tidal inundation. Mangrove trees are halophytes, capable of thriving in salty conditions, and they grow where few other trees can survive. Their presence provides a unique and irreplaceable habitat for various species, including birds, mammals, crustaceans, and fish. Furthermore, mangroves enhance water quality and mitigate pollution by filtering suspended materials and assimilating dissolved nutrients. When mangrove leaves fall into tidal waters, marine bacteria colonize them within hours, converting hard-to-digest carbon compounds into nitrogen-rich detritus.Despite growing awareness of their value, mangrove forests are under constant threat in many parts of the world, driven by economic and political motives. Although some areas protect mangroves by law, a lack of enforcement and the economic incentive to reclaim land can lead to deliberate destruction. The increasing pressure on mangrove populations and the rising levels of pollutants reaching coastal and intracoastal waters have renewed interest in understanding the crucial role of mangroves in maintaining a healthy marine ecology. Spending 1 to 2 hours in that setting was a delightful experience.

On the opposite side of the road was Eco Beach, just a two-minute walk from the mangrove walkway. With a refreshed mind, I headed to Eco Beach. This beach had earned a Blue Flag rating recently. This certification is awarded to beaches that meet specific standards, such as providing proper seating areas, restrooms, cleanliness, and safety warnings. Also, Eco Beach offered changing rooms, first aid facilities, and drinking water. The beach stretched for about 5 kilometers, and I walked along its length multiple times. Time passed quickly, and as the sun began to set, I observed an elderly couple walking along the shore, holding hands—a beautiful sight. I watched as people came and went, walking along the beach for nearly two hours.

**Sharavathi Kandla Mangrove Boardwalk: Where the roots tell the stories in silence**

Amidst the serene beauty of Eco Beach, as the sun descended and the world around me transitioned from day to night, I found myself contemplating the intricacies of human nature. It's fascinating how interconnected humans are with one another. We often perceive life as an individual journey, driven by personal choices and responsibilities. However, upon closer inspection, it becomes evident that our existence is intricately woven into a complex tapestry of interdependence.

In our daily lives, we rely on others for countless aspects, from the food we eat through the work of farmers to the clothes we wear, crafted by skilled hands, and the transportation systems that facilitate our mobility. Despite these profound connections, we sometimes become ensnared in self-centered perspectives, focusing on our own desires and aspirations.

The evening at Eco Beach allowed me to recognize that while individuality is a part of our human nature, it coexists with a profound interdependence that links us all. These reflections reminded me that our collective actions can either nurture the world we share or disrupt the delicate balance of nature.

This insight prompted me to consider how we, as individuals, can contribute to the greater good by being more conscious of our impact on the environment and the lives of others. It's a reminder that the choices we make have ripple effects that extend far beyond our immediate surroundings, and we hold the power to shape a more harmonious world for everyone.

As I lay on the beach, the lights around me began to shimmer, accentuating the wonder of the natural world. Sun dipped below the horizon, and the lights around me began to illuminate the surroundings. By around 7:30 PM, an announcement was made, politely asking people to leave the beach. I started my journey back to the homestay.

**By the shore, where the waves gently reach; Eco beach, was nature's own speech**

When I returned, I found that a family from Hyderabad had taken up residence on the same floor as mine. I engaged in a friendly conversation with them before retiring to my room.

In the morning, I informed Oliver that I would need a boat for a backwater ride the next day. Oliver provided me with the contact information of the boat operator. That concluded my day. Covered in sand from the beach, I took a refreshing bath and then fell asleep.

Around 2:30 AM, I awoke to the sound of heavy rain. It suddenly struck me that I was supposed to leave for Gokarna today, and I hadn't yet booked my accommodation. I had booked Zostel for tomorrow and Day Tripper for the following day. I checked for vacancies in the dorms and found one available at Zostel, so I secured it. As I lay in bed, tossing and turning, sleep eventually claimed me once more.

# CHAPTER SIX

# Waterside Awakening

The next day started with a surprise wake-up call at 5:15. The boat operator rang me up, urging me to be ready by 5:30 for the best sights. I hurriedly got myself together, and by 5:30, I was out the door, making my way to the boatyard right across the street. A quick note: You can rent boats for a spin from various spots in Honnavar. I chose this option as it was right across.

Now, navigating these enchanting backwaters by boat is the real deal. The boatman, who doubles as your local guide, can take you to some of the best fishing spots. These boats come in all shapes and sizes - from the traditional wooden ones to speedboats, each offering a unique charm. This place was a hidden treasure, a diamond in the rough, and it had recently gained some well-deserved attention. It is now a hotspot for pre-wedding photoshoots, giving "love at first sight" a whole new meaning.

**Honnavar Backwater #1**

As we started our journey, my eyes soaked in five distinct locales, ranging from captivating mangroves to serene lotus ponds. It was like a buffet for the senses. Everywhere I looked, there was a slice of paradise waiting to be explored. Word to the wise, the best time to hit these backwaters is when the Arabian Sea decides to throw its weight around during high tide. That's when the waterways get a massive makeover. Sunrises are preferable, offering nature's spectacular light show, as opposed to sunsets. Think of it as the universe giving you a front-row seat to the big reveal.

**Honnavar Backwater #2**

This boat trip reminded me a lot of the backwaters in Alleppey. Sharavathi backwaters were stunning, and many places could only be reached by boat. The route was super scenic and colorful, especially the narrow creeks where people lived in beautiful garden houses. With coconut trees all around and a sunset backdrop, it was incredibly peaceful and connected to nature.

**Honnavar Backwater #3**

The pièce de résistance? On the way back, there's a long bridge that offers you a heavenly view of the Sharavathi River. After two hours of rowing in heaven, it was time to go back to earth. Right when I was about to get down from the boat it started drizzling and made the river view more amazing. As the boating spot was right infront of the home, I did not add a QR code in the pictures for the address.

**Honnavar Backwater #4**

With all this adventure, it was time to head to Gokarna. But before I left Honnavar, I wanted to check out the famous hanging bridge. Sadly, it was locked up, and I couldn't get in. Bummer!

**Closed Sharavathi River Bridge**

On the road to Gokarna, I spotted an older man selling breakfast, so I stopped for a quick bite. He was 68 and had a passion for feeding people. He served me three dosas for just 25 rupees, and the sambar was top-notch.

With my belly full, I continued my journey to Mirjan Fort, where I enjoyed the pristine surroundings. The fort was surrounded by lush greenery and colorful flowers. Exploring the massive fort was a treat. It had thick walls, ruins, watchtowers, and strategic holes to shoot at enemies safely.

From the fort, I made my way to Zostel Gokarna. In the dorm, I met two friendly faces. We chatted a bit, but we skipped the name exchange. After freshening up and dropping off my laundry, I decided to unwind with a game of pool.

There, I met Raji, who complimented my Naruto Ichiraku Ramen T-shirt. We got to talking and discovered we were both from Hyderabad. She was there with a friend. She insisted that I join them on that day's adventure. While I went to my get the mobile from the room, I crossed paths with Prashanth, who was staying in the same dorm. He introduced himself as a 'worcationer' from Vizag, here to explore Gokarna with his buddies. Later, Raji, her friend and I decided to spend the day together. We planned to head to Om Beach with the intention of going on an adventurous beach trek, but our enthusiasm was quickly dampened by the scorching sun. Seeking refuge from the blazing heat, we found ourselves at Namaste Cafe, where we swapped stories about our backgrounds and work.

Later, as the sun began to set, we watched the spectacular sight of Om Beach from a rocky perch. Afterward, as we headed back to Zostel, Raji asked me if I'd be willing to accompany her on a late-night mission: to drop off her friend at the bus stand. I agreed and headed to the dorm room.

Now, the room was deserted, so I decided to take a quick nap. Meanwhile, downstairs, the common area was alive with people having a blast, playing a game of UNO. I couldn't resist the temptation, so I joined in.

My two dorm mates from the morning were also part of the action, and we engaged in a lively game. We played for a while, but eventually, the call to sleep became irresistible. So, I slipped back into my room and dozed off.

Around 11:30 PM, my phone rang, and it was Raji on the line. They were about to set off. I struggled out of my half-asleep state, and we hopped into an auto to drop off her friend. Mission accomplished, we were heading back when we got pulled over by the police. The officers, with curiosity piqued, asked us where we'd been. We offered an honest explanation, and after a quick once-over, they waved us on.

Back at Zostel, I surrendered to the beckoning arms of slumber once more. Ah, what a day! But wait, there's more to the story. When I returned to the room, I saw the friend I had chatted with earlier that morning. Her name was Kanchi, and she was an architect from Mumbai. To my surprise, she was actually the sister of the other person I had met in the morning. Our conversation meandered through various topics, including their journey to Honnavar. As the clock inched towards 1:45, we bid each other goodnight and drifted into the peaceful embrace of sleep. What an eventful day it had been!

@Gokarna dump

# CHAPTER SEVEN

# Journeys Beyond, Conversations Within

I woke up early to the soothing sound of beach waves. The dorm was still asleep, so I quickly got ready and hit the streets of Gokarna. It felt like stepping back into the '90s with a vintage vibe all around. In the market street, I met a man in his 70s, and we had a chat for about 45 minutes. His stories painted a vibrant mural of his childhood, life, and friendships. We even took a picture together before saying goodbye.

By 8:30 AM, the tempting aroma of Dattaprasad Tiffin Canteen led me to the car street. This humble spot, run by a Brahmin family, offered authentic South Indian breakfast. The crispy masala dosas and fluffy idlis were a delight, and even the sparrows seemed to approve as they chirped around.

After a visit to the Ganesh temple, I bought a "dothi" to wear for my visit to the Mahabaleshwar temple the next day. Only those in traditional dress are allowed inside. On my way back to Zostel, I noticed a Shiva graffiti and started taking pictures when it suddenly started raining. I found shelter in an old man's home, who turned out to be the head priest of the Gokarna temple.

For half an hour, rain danced on the roof as I observed three school friends boarding a bus under umbrellas—a nostalgic scene from my school days. When the rain eased, I made my way back to Zostel, preparing for the journey to Yana Caves.

**Vintage and graffiti vibes only please ;)**

While starting my bike, I encountered Raji in the common area. She inquired about my plans, expressing her desire to visit Murudeshwar. Since she couldn't find transportation, we decided to go together, planning to visit Yana Caves from there. Our Murudeshwar trip included a visit to the less crowded Gopuram top, offering a breathtaking view of synchronized waves hitting the shore.

**Aerial view @Murudeshwar**

We then set off to Yana. We stopped for lunch at a local shop on the way where we met Ms. Kitten sleeping peacefully. The journey amidst intermittent rain was mesmerizing. The lush green trees and the sunlight filtering through created a breathtaking scene. Reaching Yana, a 45-minute trek led to the colossal caves. At the entry, we took blessings of the god Bhairaveshwara. We then took a few steps to enter the cave where the bats welcomed us into a natural wonder. As the sun began to set, casting a gentle drizzle, the caves revealed a spectacle beyond words. Nature's artistry, illuminated by the play of light and rain, left me in awe.

Exiting the cave, a simple yet profound sight awaited—raindrops falling on a rock's sharp edge, creating miniature cascades. Such moments, I thought, are the whispers of divinity in the ordinary.

# YANA CAVES #1

Ameowwzing nature till Yana Caves!!

**Bliss!**

At the parking area around 4:30 PM, I realized our phones were out of charge, and we didn't have power banks. The plan to visit Vibhuthi Falls was dropped, and we headed back to Zostel.

After freshening up, I met a new person in the dorm, said hi, and joined others in the common area. I got to know Kanchi's sister, Anushka, who happens to be a lawyer. While chatting, Raji introduced a new friend, Emima, from her dorm. Emima is a second-year nursing student from Mangalore. It's nice to see more young people exploring travel early on, and gaining diverse perspectives.

We resumed our UNO game, which then shifted to spooky stories. I remember Anushka suggesting a midnight stargazing plan from a nearby spot. However, Google hinted at rain and clouds, so we decided to wait and see.

Kanchi shared a funny tale of their "paddy field adventure" earlier in the day, making their way through muddy fields to reach "Chez Christophe."

Then, we dove into horror stories, with me recounting childhood and hostel tales, Kanchi sharing an incident from her architectural project, and Anushka telling a gripping story from her time in Delhi. Some found the stories puzzling, but I enjoyed pondering the mysteries they unveiled.

As the hostel manager signaled the end of our gathering due to lights-out, Kanchi took a phone call, and some friends continued partying. Emima and Raji headed to the dorm, while Anushka and I engaged in what I felt, an intellectual conversation. Our conversation expanded to human perspectives, contemplating our unique ability to perceive the world. I drew parallels with how animals see things differently due to their vision, introducing the idea of an unseen world next to ours. The musings turned into a simple exploration of ghosts and paranormal activities. We then discussed about our professions, politics, talked about dark magic, human emotions, and tried to dissect the perspectives of the current generation's mindset. A range of captivating subjects indeed.

Approaching 1:30 AM, we thought of continuing our conversation in the dorm. However, the dorm was silent. We chose a whispered good night, considering potential disturbance, and settled into a restful sleep. Zzz... Zzz...

# CHAPTER EIGHT

# Cafe Chronicles: Conversations Beyond Midnight

I woke up the next day with the anticipation of heading to Trippr. Excitement bubbled within me, eager to discover what Trippr had in store. Surprisingly, Raji and Emima also secured rooms there, as Zostel was fully booked. Upon arriving at Trippr, the distinct vibe immediately struck me—it was right on the shore. Although the check-in time was 12, we waited in the common area. While Raji and Emima sorted out their dorm booking with the property manager, I glimpsed a few faces, offering smiles. I approached a guy working on his laptop, Sriram from Chennai, a fellow solo traveler on a workation. We chatted in Tamil, surprising him with my language skills. Another traveler from Bangalore joined our conversation.

After freshening up in our dorm, I visited the Mahabaleshwar temple, a significant pilgrimage site among Hindus. The temple's 1500-year-old Shivling, intricately carved into the walls, exuded a Varanasi-like aura. Immersed in the divine peace, I returned to the room before heading to the common area for breakfast.

**Trippr's trace and Mahabaleshwar's sacred embrace**

Observing Raji, Emima, and a new face, Tharun from Bangalore conversing, I awaited my food. A playful puppy joined me, adding a delightful touch to our breakfast. In the common area, a group invited me to play volleyball on the shore. Me and Sriram joined in, and time swiftly transitioned to the afternoon. Back at the dorm, I met a 30-year-old from Bangalore who conversed in Tamil with Sriram. The afternoon drew me back to Zostel, where I connected with new friends from Mysore and Pune.

Anushka and Kanchi extended a warm invitation to chill at the shacks on Kudle Beach. We invited Raji to join us, and we planned to visit Kudle. However, the beach was poorly maintained, prompting a change of plans to go to "Chez Christophe." We immersed ourselves in the ambiance of the restaurant, losing track of time until around 6 PM. Concerned about Tharun and Emima's safety in the dark and rain, we attempted to call them without success. We resumed our conversation, meeting Ms. Nasa, a recent employee at the cafe. She was a delight to talk to.

Around 7:30 PM, Tharun and Emima called, reassuring us of their safe return to the dorm. Discovering that Anushka's birthday was the next day, we debated celebrating at the cafe but decided against it due to safety concerns and ongoing celebrations at Zostel. Despite having bikes, I chose not to join them as I had plans to travel to Sirisi and Dhavangere the next day. We opted to stay a bit longer at the cafe, foregoing the live concert at Zostel.

We requested Anoop, the cafe manager, for some cards to play. The auto arrived, and it was time for Kanchi and Anushka to bid us farewell. We sent them off with warm birthday wishes for Anushka.

With the remaining trio—Tharun, Emima, and Raji—I continued chatting in the cafe. Our conversation touched on various topics, from anime and music to our professions and future plans. Tharun and I even delved into personal matters, discussing family situations.

Before we knew it, it was 1:45 AM, and we were surprised at how quickly time had flown. Anoop expressed his gratitude as we left, and we discussed the inception of the cafe. He mentioned the possibility of offering an internship and shared plans for constructing accommodations, expected to be ready in a couple of months—a promising opportunity to earn, relax, and connect with people.

**Bonding over breakfast with my sophisticated friend, the gourmet pup. Then, the whole day of dining with a side of tales and endless conversations at Chez Christophe.**

We returned to Trippr around 2 AM and stumbled upon someone celebrating a birthday. Joining in the festivities, we wished for a joyous year ahead.

When I met Sriram in the afternoon in the room, he inquired about joining me on my journey back to Bangalore, and I gladly agreed. However, upon returning, I couldn't find him in bed. I messaged him about our early departure plans for the morning.

Engaging in a late-night conversation with Emima, she shared family photos, and we discussed our mutual passion for writing quotes. With a wedding to attend the next day, we also explored the best commuting options for her. Before retiring, I plugged in my gadgets for charging and quickly drifted into sleep as I settled onto the bed.

# CHAPTER NINE

# Homeward Trails

The next morning, I woke up to find Sriram missing in his bed. A quick call brought him there in 10 minutes. We kickstarted the day with a coffee at the road's end before heading to Sri Marikamba Temple in Sirsi. The journey, surrounded by lush greenery, was a visual treat. Arriving near the temple, we secured a room to freshen up, took a bath, and proceeded to explore the temple. Adorned with unique murals in Kaavi art, the temple's cloisters featured depictions of Hindu deities, with a central image of the serene form of Goddess Durga riding a tiger and defeating a demon. The smiling 7-foot-tall idol exuded a tranquil charm.

**With Sri Ram @Sri Marikamba Temple**

Eager to partake in the free lunch offered by the temple in the afternoon, we realized we were an hour early early, and the lunch service would begin at 12. So, we decided to move on to our next destination - the Sahasralinga River. We had mangalore buns and puri for brunch on a road side shop on the way. The journey was serene, with both Sriram and I taking breaks to absorb the beauty of nature. We met a stranger with a bike breakdown and we decided to offer an assistance with our toolkit. Unfortunately, it couldn't repair the accelerator cable. Continuing our journey, we reached the Sahasralinga River, where we marveled at the surroundings, crossed a bridge, and explored the area on foot. The site, known for its 1000 Shiva Lingas, carved along the Shalmala's banks, held a mysterious and breathtaking allure. Each of these lingas was also accompanied by carvings of Nandi, the bull.

**Awsome breakfast followed by a peaceful time @Sahasralinga River**

The road ahead wasn't smooth, but the beauty of nature persisted. As Sriram had plans to return to Chennai, we decided to push through to Bangalore without stopping in Davangere for the famous Benne dosa. Originally, the plan was to stay in Davangere and enjoy the benne dosa the next morning. However, with this plan, I thought of resting at home instead. The journey until before Davangere was tiresome due to poor road conditions. A rest stop near a toll gate provided some relief, with the chatty shopkeeper Shruti offering good company. By 6:30, we reached the outskirts of Bangalore amidst the rain, with the fatigue from the day's drive setting in.

The primary goal now was to get home quickly. Anticipating a 10 PM arrival, I considered meeting Sriram in Bangalore city due to traffic constraints. As I approached Mahadevpura, a sudden realization struck - I needed to collect my room key from a friend in Marathalli. I left it with him concerned about losing it during the journey. I called him only to find he was in his hometown. A colleague in Varthur came to the rescue, and I spent the night there. Around half an hour later, Sriram informed me of his safe arrival at a friend's place, where he planned to stay for two days before heading to Chennai. Reflecting on the last 10 days of my life, I felt a sense of pride and accomplishment. I drifted into sleep, proud of the journey I had successfully completed.

**Last picture clicked on the trip: Davangere-Bangalore highway**

# Echoes Of The Journey

As I stand at the crossroads of the familiar, the echoes of the road resonate within me—a symphony composed of discovery, friendship, and introspection. Every encounter, a thread woven into the fabric of my being, a testament to the profound connections we forge in this journey called life. The places I've touched, the faces I've met, are etched into my soul. The road is not just a physical path; it mirrors the intricate journey of life itself.

In these closing lines, I share a realization—a reminder that time is a fleeting companion. Our lifespan is a mere fraction of eternity, and every interaction leaves a thread in the tapestry of memory. Life's brevity underscores the importance of embracing the moments, seizing opportunities, and weaving a life rich with experiences.

Consider the arithmetic of existence. The routine of an average life—a childhood, a career, weekends of respite—narrows our active years. Subtracting moments spent in the ebb and flow of daily life, we're left with a finite number of days. A stark reminder to live deliberately, for time, once spent, is irretrievable.

As the pages turn, I urge you not to merely exist but to live profoundly. The road has taught me that life is a delicate balance of joy and pain. Embrace both, for they are inseparable companions on this journey. Don't be afraid to dive into the depths of human experience, to share your joys, your pains, and your most authentic self.

In the embrace of travel, I've witnessed proposals, celebrated weddings, and confronted fears with newfound friends. The road is a testament to the resilience of the human spirit, its capacity to find joy amid pain, and the enduring connections formed on the path less traveled.

One crucial lesson resonates—the pace of your journey is uniquely yours. Don't measure your progress against others; we each walk our distinct paths. Recognize the immense power you hold to impact the world. A listening ear, a compassionate heart—simple gestures that can make a profound difference.

In life, every thread matters. As you read these words, may you be inspired to live authentically, to spread joy, and to pursue your passions fearlessly. Life is fleeting, and regrets weigh heavier than untraveled roads.

I could continue, for the journey's tales are boundless. If you feel the urge to share, to connect, know that the road has taught me the value of genuine human connection and you know how to reach out to me. Cheers to life, where every detour is a scenic route, and every wrong turn leads to a surprising adventure!